365 Things Every Couple Should Know

DOUG FIELDS

HARVEST HOUSE PUBLISHERS
Eugene, Oregon 97402

Scripture quoted from The Everyday Bible, New Century Version, copyright © 1987, 1988 by Word Publishing, Nashville, TN 37214. Used by permission.

Cover by Koechel Peterson & Associates, Minneapolis, Minnesota

Published in association with the literary agency of Alive Communications, Inc., 7680 Goddard Street, Suite 200, Colorado Springs, CO 80920

365 THINGS EVERY COUPLE SHOULD KNOW

Copyright © 1993 by Doug Fields
Published by Harvest House Publishers
Eugene, Oregon 97402

ISBN 0-7369-0697-5

Printed in the United States of America

02 03 04 05 06 / BC-CF / 10 9 8 7 6 5 4 3

To Marv & Elva:
Thank you for being a superb example
of what 50 years of marriage should be.

Introduction

If you're single or already a couple, *365 Things Every Couple Should Know* is only the beginning of the many ways you can say (to your mate), "I love you" and "I appreciate you."

Making daily deposits into your relational bank account assures you a high rate of return. Most deposits only take an extra moment or two, but the rewards are forever...and they're so easy you'l wonder, "Why didn't I think of that?"

Enjoy.

Doug Fields

1

Every Couple Should Know...

to embrace
one another
for no reason.

2

Every Couple Should Know...

how to affirm your
love by giving your spouse
a homemade surprise.

Every Couple Should Know...

God's love for your spouse has no conditions.

Every Couple Should Know...

it is easier to complain about a fault than to forgive one.

Every Couple Should Know...

the qualities within your spouse
that ignited your interest
when you first met.

Every Couple Should Know...

Eve was created
to be a queen.

Every Couple Should Know...

Adam was created
to be a king.

Every Couple Should Know...

a good surprise is to have
your spouse's car washed.

Every Couple Should Know...

how to give your spouse
a visible expression of love.

Every Couple Should Know...

there's no time
like the present to begin
bettering your marriage.

11

Every Couple Should Know...

how to take a 30-minute vacation.

12

Every Couple Should Know...

how to ensure your criticisms are constructive and not destructive.

13

Every Couple Should Know...

laughter at a spouse's failure
doesn't motivate change.

14

Every Couple Should Know...

it is fun to be spontaneous:
tickle, dance, or join
your spouse in the shower.

Every Couple Should Know...

when to abandon
housework for play.

Every Couple Should Know...

not to reprimand in public
and double the damage.

17

Every Couple Should Know...

the importance of looking
into your spouse's eyes
while listening.

18

Every Couple Should Know...

that God cares more
about your marriage
than you do.

19

Every Couple Should Know...

when to add
an unanticipated pleasure
to your daily regimen.

20

Every Couple Should Know...

your children
will love to hear
your courtship stories.

Every Couple Should Know...

to always compliment
the cook.

Every Couple Should Know...

a failed attempt at romance
should be countered
with sincere appreciation.

23

Every Couple Should Know...

God has a different
standard of beauty
than we do.

24

Every Couple Should Know...

the fun shouldn't end
at the wedding.

25

Every Couple Should Know...

to cherish the rare moments of uncontrollable laughter.

26

Every Couple Should Know...

one compliment a day isn't too many.

27

Every Couple Should Know...

how to
"give preference to
one another in honor"
(Romans 12:10).

28

Every Couple Should Know...

how to nurture
your spouse's potential.

Every Couple Should Know...

"I love you"
sounds much better than
"Why didn't you?"

30

Every Couple Should Know...

how to bring out
the playful child
in one another.

Every Couple Should Know...

years will steal beauty from
the body but true attraction
will delight in aging flesh.

Every Couple Should Know...

empathy is
much more attractive
than apathy.

Every Couple Should Know...

good memories are priceless
no matter what they cost.

Every Couple Should Know...

the importance
of discovering insight
from every problem.

35

Every Couple Should Know...

your spouse has
positive qualities that
you should affirm regularly.

36

Every Couple Should Know...

how to write your spouse
a 20-word love note.

Every Couple Should Know...

how to turn *off* the TV
and *on* the communication.

38

Every Couple Should Know...

to not yell at one another
unless the house is on fire.

39

Every Couple Should Know...

when to break
the diet restrictions
and pig out.

40

Every Couple Should Know...

your spouse's
secret dream.

Every Couple Should Know...

the winner
of the conflict
isn't always the winner.

Every Couple Should Know...

the importance
of courtship
after marriage.

43

Every Couple Should Know...

please and *thank you*
are not just
for children to say.

44

Every Couple Should Know...

how to make
your spouse laugh.

Every Couple Should Know...

positive memories
become anchors
for future storms.

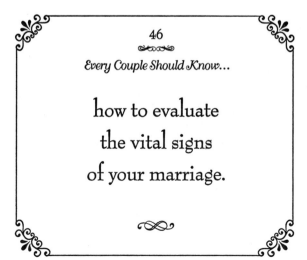

Every Couple Should Know...

how to evaluate
the vital signs
of your marriage.

47

Every Couple Should Know…

where to go
when you are free
for 24 hours.

48

Every Couple Should Know…

one way to show that you care
is by spending your spare time
with your spouse.

Every Couple Should Know...

how to save
for a rainy day.

Every Couple Should Know...

the difference between
what makes your spouse
tick and ticked-off.

51

Every Couple Should Know...

how to give your spouse
a "second wind."

52

Every Couple Should Know...

showering together
saves water.

Every Couple Should Know...

a day without
"I love you"
is a wasted day.

Every Couple Should Know...

how to cook
your spouse's
favorite meal.

55

Every Couple Should Know...

major house projects
may need to be followed
by minor marital counseling.

56

Every Couple Should Know...

the importance
of maintaining
sexual attraction.

57

Every Couple Should Know...

how to make
a homemade greeting card
for a special occasion.

∞

58

Every Couple Should Know...

when to take over
responsibilities and let your
spouse enjoy a bubble bath.

Every Couple Should Know...

how to use a camera
and photo album to
document your relationship.

∞

Every Couple Should Know...

a few massage
techniques.

∞

61

Every Couple Should Know...

the fun of buying a unique gift
your spouse would never buy
for himself or herself.

62

Every Couple Should Know...

to forget your
wedding-day waist size.

63

Every Couple Should Know...

a board game, two candles,
and a fireplace can help create
a romantic home date.

64

Every Couple Should Know...

your spouse's
favorite magazine.

Every Couple Should Know...

the simple intimacy
of holding hands.

Every Couple Should Know...

the importance of having
a "Do Not Disturb" sign.

Every Couple Should Know...

a bird feeder can become
a backyard theater.

Every Couple Should Know...

at least one dining location
that encourages you
to dress up.

Every Couple Should Know...

to celebrate
the little things
in your lives.

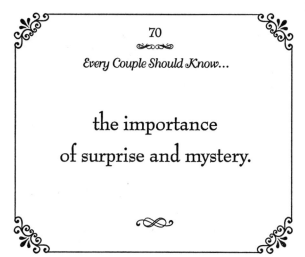

Every Couple Should Know...

the importance
of surprise and mystery.

Every Couple Should Know...

the best
sunset-watching location
and frequent it.

Every Couple Should Know...

how to celebrate
your spouse's victories.

73

Every Couple Should Know...

to not replace
the evening gown
with a bathrobe.

74

Every Couple Should Know...

to not replace
a night on the town
with a television show.

Every Couple Should Know...

marriage creates situations
that should induce laughter
rather than anger.

Every Couple Should Know...

your spouse's
favorite music.

77

Every Couple Should Know...

it is important (and fun)
to save love letters.

78

Every Couple Should Know...

when it is time to do
something together to
escape immediate pressures.

Every Couple Should Know...

a romantic location
within walking distance
from your home.

Every Couple Should Know...

the game of Scrabble
has been known to ignite
major arguments.

81

Every Couple Should Know...

their own intimate vocabulary
(which is foreign to
other family members).

82

Every Couple Should Know...

the joy of popcorn,
photo albums,
and old music.

Every Couple Should Know...

it is immature to run
through the sprinklers...
but lots of fun.

Every Couple Should Know...

touch is a powerful form
of communication.

85

Every Couple Should Know...

it is fun to discover
short love notes
around the house.

86

Every Couple Should Know...

to be on the lookout
for a creative gift
to express your love.

87

Every Couple Should Know…

how to travel together without fighting.

88

Every Couple Should Know…

how to pamper your spouse.

Every Couple Should Know...

a quality marriage isn't measured
by how few problems you have
but by how you handle
the problems.

Every Couple Should Know...

at least one form
of exercise
you can do together.

91

Every Couple Should Know...

a trip to the local library
isn't as boring
as it might sound.

92

Every Couple Should Know...

TV executives don't care about
marriage communication...
divorce means
more TV purchases.

93

Every Couple Should Know...

a cheerful heart
is good medicine
(Proverbs 17:22).

94

Every Couple Should Know...

unexpected gifts can
bring great pleasure.

Every Couple Should Know...

a good marriage
is the best gift
you can give your children.

Every Couple Should Know...

marriage should have
more dreams
than nightmares.

Every Couple Should Know...

God has written a love
letter (the Bible) filled with
great principles for marriage.

Every Couple Should Know...

your spouse wants
to be viewed as attractive.

Every Couple Should Know…

to take lots of pictures
during your vacations.

Every Couple Should Know…

there is no easy answer
to marriage problems.

Every Couple Should Know...

Eve probably said,
"God, Adam just
doesn't understand."

Every Couple Should Know...

it's easier to exercise
when it's fun.

Every Couple Should Know...

love and marriage
go together like
a horse and carriage.

Every Couple Should Know...

if sensitivity
had a price tag
it would be expensive.

Every Couple Should Know...

biblical writers refer
to the act of sex
as "to know."

Every Couple Should Know...

Moses got married
and "knew" his wife
for a year without working.

107

Every Couple Should Know...

a good listener
hears between the lines.

108

Every Couple Should Know...

to buy your spouse
crazy underwear every year.

Every Couple Should Know...

hints and innuendos
can sometimes be
subtle forms of manipulation.

Every Couple Should Know...

to eat cookie dough in bed
at least once a year.

Every Couple Should Know...

verbal intercourse
is more important
than the other type.

Every Couple Should Know...

how to have fun
without money.

113

Every Couple Should Know...

you should keep your
spouse's insecurities private.

⚮

114

Every Couple Should Know...

it is okay
to let your spouse
take the credit.

⚮

115

Every Couple Should Know...

the correct answer to
"Do you love me?" is not,
"I married you, didn't I?"

116

Every Couple Should Know...

to save your spouse's
handmade gifts
and cards.

117

Every Couple Should Know...

the difference between
sex and love.

118

Every Couple Should Know...

a quick phone call when
you're going to be late can
defuse a potential explosion.

119

Every Couple Should Know...

marriages are built on
small expressions
of affection.

120

Every Couple Should Know...

to not give up...
miracles do happen.

121

Every Couple Should Know...

to return kindness
to one another.

122

Every Couple Should Know...

there are few shortcuts
to genuine intimacy.

123

Every Couple Should Know...

how to make
your spouse feel
like a million bucks!

124

Every Couple Should Know...

divorce wasn't
in God's plan
when He created marriage.

Every Couple Should Know...

how to establish
realistic expectations.

Every Couple Should Know...

how to give your spouse
a sense of dignity.

Every Couple Should Know...

to apply God's definition
of love to your marriage
(see 1 Corinthians 13:4-7).

Every Couple Should Know...

childhood wounds
are not easily healed.

129

Every Couple Should Know...

when to escape
to an environment
for undivided attention.

130

Every Couple Should Know...

comments about
physical features
that can't be changed
are a waste of breath.

Every Couple Should Know...

how to cherish
and respect one another.

Every Couple Should Know...

how to remain
the "best catch"
for your spouse.

Every Couple Should Know...

when the warning light is on,
it's time to stop, check the engine,
and make adjustments.

Every Couple Should Know...

anger is not
intrinsically evil...
resentment is.

135

Every Couple Should Know...

how to take responsibility
for your actions instead of
blaming your spouse.

136

Every Couple Should Know...

how to ignite passion.

Every Couple Should Know...

how to face
stressful events
peacefully.

138

Every Couple Should Know...

the importance of being
straightforward about getting
your needs met and refraining
from manipulation.

Every Couple Should Know...

to recall constantly
what first attracted you
to your spouse.

Every Couple Should Know...

true forgiveness
goes beyond words
to action.

141

Every Couple Should Know...

how to stick together
when your world
falls apart.

142

Every Couple Should Know...

there are some things
about your spouse
you simply cannot change.

Every Couple Should Know...

the attractiveness
of a positive attitude.

Every Couple Should Know...

it's okay to read a book
or take a course
on improving your marriage.

145

Every Couple Should Know...

the value of hugging
your spouse daily.

146

Every Couple Should Know...

to pray
for one another.

Every Couple Should Know...

anger impairs judgment
and provokes
harmful words.

Every Couple Should Know...

a walk together
is good for both
the heart and the soul.

Every Couple Should Know...

marriage is more than
a relationship; it's a skill
that needs to be learned.

Every Couple Should Know...

to speak well of your
spouse—in his or her
presence *and* absence.

151

Every Couple Should Know…

physical intimacy is
easier to achieve
than emotional intimacy.

152

Every Couple Should Know…

the nonnegotiables
in your marriage.

153

Every Couple Should Know...

to cut the edge
off your tongue.

154

Every Couple Should Know...

behaviors that
please your partner.

Every Couple Should Know...

money problems are
a major cause
for divorce.

Every Couple Should Know...

a woman is capable
of becoming
more sexually responsive.

Every Couple Should Know...

a man is capable
of becoming more attentive.

Every Couple Should Know...

small steps
in the right direction
can produce big results.

159

Every Couple Should Know...

"do not let the sun
go down on your anger"
(Ephesians 4:26).

160

Every Couple Should Know...

to have a
regular date night.

Every Couple Should Know...

ignored problems
will not become solved
on their own.

Every Couple Should Know...

how to express
laughter and humor
on a daily basis.

163

Every Couple Should Know...

how to be a good loser.

164

Every Couple Should Know...

to save
your favorite memories
in a journal.

165

Every Couple Should Know...

to celebrate Thanksgiving
more than once a year.

166

Every Couple Should Know...

the importance
of viewing problems
from an alternate viewpoint.

167

Every Couple Should Know...

never is an ugly word.

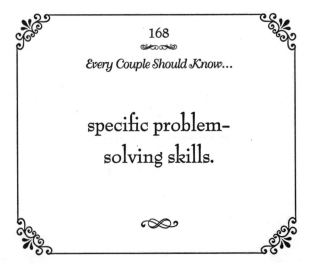

168

Every Couple Should Know...

specific problem-
solving skills.

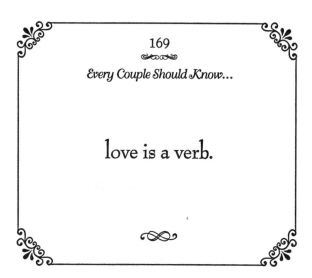

Every Couple Should Know...

love is a verb.

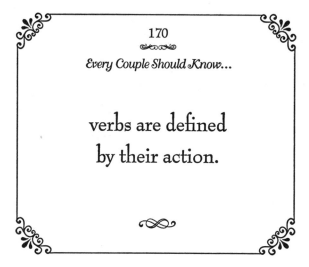

Every Couple Should Know...

verbs are defined
by their action.

Every Couple Should Know...

how to keep
your spouse from becoming
just a roommate.

Every Couple Should Know...

to dream big together.

173

Every Couple Should Know...

how to feel comfortable
saying "no" to your
spouse's request for sex.

174

Every Couple Should Know...

how to pinpoint the real issues
of conflict and avoid
blaming one another.

175

Every Couple Should Know...

sex doesn't have to
be great every time.

176

Every Couple Should Know...

the value of creating
a safe environment to
openly share your feelings.

177

Every Couple Should Know...

change begins
with oneself.

178

Every Couple Should Know...

quality dialogue every day
has great rewards.

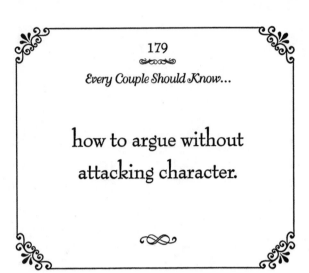

179

Every Couple Should Know...

how to argue without
attacking character.

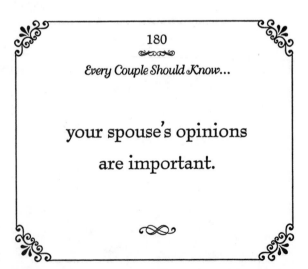

180

Every Couple Should Know...

your spouse's opinions
are important.

181

Every Couple Should Know...

the importance of
being able to talk
comfortably about sex.

182

Every Couple Should Know...

how to turn a negative thought
into a positive statement
before the brain
engages the mouth.

183

Every Couple Should Know...

a sensuous kiss a day
keeps the blood flowing.

184

Every Couple Should Know...

"Fine" is not the answer
for the question,
"How are you feeling?"

185

Every Couple Should Know...

it is better to help
your partner be on time
instead of blaming him or her
for being late.

186

Every Couple Should Know...

how to communicate feelings
during sexual activity.

187

Every Couple Should Know...

how to interpret
your spouse's
nonverbal communication.

188

Every Couple Should Know...

both partners are equally
involved in creating
the good and bad
of a marriage.

189

Every Couple Should Know...

how to live
beneath their means.

190

Every Couple Should Know...

an encouraging relationship
begins when you
look for the positives
about your partner.

191

Every Couple Should Know...

your spouse's
clothing sizes.

192

Every Couple Should Know...

touch is a powerful way
to express concern
and appreciation.

Every Couple Should Know...

the silent treatment
was invented
by a kindergartner.

Every Couple Should Know...

the importance of
each other's individuality.

Every Couple Should Know...

how to avoid
the same sexual routine.

Every Couple Should Know...

how to give
a compliment
without adding a qualifier.

197

Every Couple Should Know...

it is fun to switch roles
when it comes to
initiation of sex, dates,
buying groceries, etc.

198

Every Couple Should Know...

how to complete this
sentence to your spouse:
"I love you because..."

199

Every Couple Should Know...

when to forgive
and how to forget.

200

Every Couple Should Know...

how to flirt
with each other.

201

Every Couple Should Know...

happily married people
do exist.

202

Every Couple Should Know...

a few simple
ground rules
for resolving conflict.

203

Every Couple Should Know...

the fun of
a new activity.

204

Every Couple Should Know...

how to
mutually participate
in decision making.

205

Every Couple Should Know...

how to appreciate
and accept the differences
in your partner.

206

Every Couple Should Know...

to remember your anniversary
without subtle reminders
from your spouse.

207

Every Couple Should Know...

sex is not
a four-letter word.

208

Every Couple Should Know...

patience...
and how to exercise it.

209

Every Couple Should Know...

to find humor
in negative situations.

210

Every Couple Should Know...

intimacy
can be expressed
without sex and passion.

211

Every Couple Should Know…

what to do
when your marriage
is no longer
a top priority.

212

Every Couple Should Know…

to snuggle in front
of a fireplace.

213

Every Couple Should Know...

the importance
of planning fun
into your schedule.

214

Every Couple Should Know...

it is okay
to agree to disagree.

Every Couple Should Know...

mature love
is partner-centered.

Every Couple Should Know...

to slow dance
in your underwear...
in private.

217

Every Couple Should Know...

the difference between
liking your spouse
and loving him or her.

218

Every Couple Should Know...

to be proud when
introducing your mate.

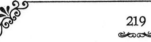

219

Every Couple Should Know...

how to view life
from your partner's shoes.

220

Every Couple Should Know...

how to spell
f-l-e-x-i-b-i-l-i-t-y.

Every Couple Should Know...

females tend
to perceive emotions
better than males.

Every Couple Should Know...

how to comfort
the fears of your spouse.

223

Every Couple Should Know...

to attack and conquer
crises as a team.

224

Every Couple Should Know...

to not let kids dictate
your marriage relationship.

225

Every Couple Should Know...

sex begins

in the morning

by the way you talk to

and treat one another.

226

Every Couple Should Know...

it is terrible to have to

seek approval

from your spouse.

Every Couple Should Know...

women cry five times
more than men.

Every Couple Should Know...

how to move from
competition to cooperation.

229

Every Couple Should Know...

sticks and stones
are much less painful
than words carelessly spoken.

230

Every Couple Should Know...

men reach their sexual peak
at about age 20;
women at about age 35.

231

Every Couple Should Know...

marriage is a
collision of two worlds.

232

Every Couple Should Know...

to appreciate
your spouse's occupation.

233

Every Couple Should Know...

the hurt that is caused
when you fail
to keep your promises.

234

Every Couple Should Know...

how to make wisdom
a marriage partner.

235

Every Couple Should Know...

to avoid
trivial arguments.

236

Every Couple Should Know...

to express gratefulness
for met needs.

237

Every Couple Should Know...

how to say,
"I'm sorry."

238

Every Couple Should Know...

women's friendships
are typically deeper
than men's.

Every Couple Should Know...

a quality marriage is built
with two people
good at forgiveness.

Every Couple Should Know...

you must remove the plank
in your own eye
before pointing out
the speck in your partner's.

241

Every Couple Should Know...

encouragement before marriage
is kindness,
but encouragement after marriage
is a necessity.

242

Every Couple Should Know...

to not expect
overnight miracles.

243

Every Couple Should Know...

how to agree more
and argue less.

244

Every Couple Should Know...

being the right person
is more important than
trying to change your spouse
into the right person.

Every Couple Should Know...

marriage is more enjoyable
when neither of you
cares who wins.

Every Couple Should Know...

how to serve God
together.

Every Couple Should Know...

it is not the number of years
you are married that counts
but what you do
during those years.

Every Couple Should Know...

how to make
every anniversary
a special celebration.

249

Every Couple Should Know...

it is better
to stress *what* is right
instead of *who* is right.

250

Every Couple Should Know...

how to openly communicate
sexual desires.

251

Every Couple Should Know...

to read
Song of Solomon
together.

252

Every Couple Should Know...

to save
pleasant thoughts
and good memories
as much as money.

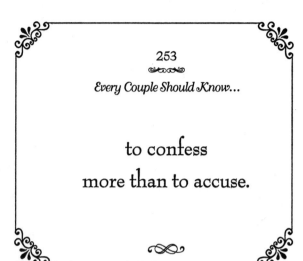

253

Every Couple Should Know...

to confess
more than to accuse.

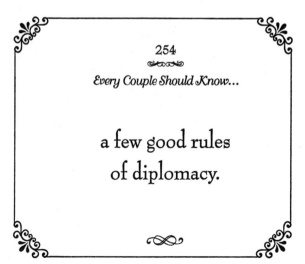

254

Every Couple Should Know...

a few good rules
of diplomacy.

255

Every Couple Should Know...

going the extra mile
will burn 400 calories.

256

Every Couple Should Know...

"a soft answer
turns away wrath"
(Proverbs 15:1).

Every Couple Should Know...

perfection simply
is not possible.

Every Couple Should Know...

how to pretend
no one else is alive
when you are being
romantic with your spouse.

259

Every Couple Should Know...

to schedule
your mid-life crisis.

260

Every Couple Should Know...

good communication
is vital to long-term
sexual fulfillment.

Every Couple Should Know...

recognition and praise
from a spouse is sweeter
than from anyone else.

Every Couple Should Know...

to bathe in optimism.

Every Couple Should Know...

divorce is
to the emotions
what death is to the soul.

Every Couple Should Know...

it is better to be
solution-conscious
rather than problem-oriented.

265

Every Couple Should Know...

sex is a privilege!

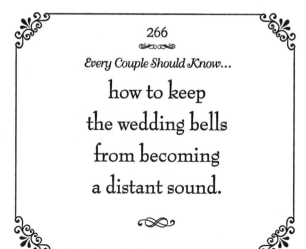

266

Every Couple Should Know...

how to keep
the wedding bells
from becoming
a distant sound.

267

Every Couple Should Know...

the importance of a weekly
meeting to discuss problems,
family, calendar, goals,
finances, and so on.

268

Every Couple Should Know...

a growing marriage
gets stronger and better
over the years.

269

Every Couple Should Know...

to listen
more than talk.

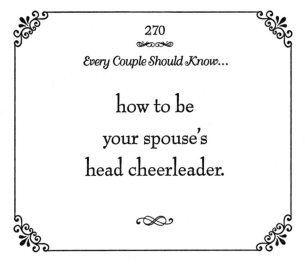

270

Every Couple Should Know...

how to be
your spouse's
head cheerleader.

271

Every Couple Should Know...

romance isn't tied
to just anniversaries
and Valentine's Day.

272

Every Couple Should Know...

the past is past...
move on.

273

Every Couple Should Know...

a healthy marriage
precedes
a healthy family.

274

Every Couple Should Know...

the pleasure
of recalling
the fun you had
before you were married.

275

Every Couple Should Know...

to not use humor
at your spouse's expense.

276

Every Couple Should Know...

some nearby scenic spots
you can visit to
appreciate God's creation.

Every Couple Should Know...

the strongest marriages
move beyond lovers
to best friends.

Every Couple Should Know...

how to spoil
your spouse.

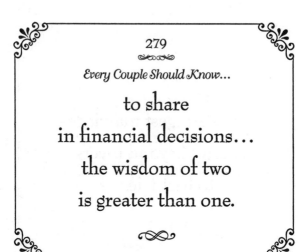

279

Every Couple Should Know…

to share
in financial decisions…
the wisdom of two
is greater than one.

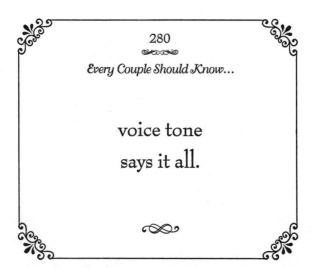

280

Every Couple Should Know…

voice tone
says it all.

281

Every Couple Should Know...

the strength
of gentleness.

282

Every Couple Should Know...

it takes only
a second to smile,
but the impression you make
can last for hours.

283

Every Couple Should Know...

an exemplary marriage is
the best type of preaching
your children will ever
hear and see.

284

Every Couple Should Know...

orgasm isn't the name
of a biblical city.

285

Every Couple Should Know...

to kiss
when stuck in traffic.

286

Every Couple Should Know...

Ephesians 5:22,28 in a nutshell:
Husbands, love your wife
as yourself and wives,
respect your husband.

287

to greet your spouse with
an affectionate welcome
when he or she comes home.

288

when your spouse needs to hear
she is beautiful
or he is handsome.

289

Every Couple Should Know...

God created
sexual desire.

290

Every Couple Should Know...

reliving past disputes
is a sign of
nonforgiveness.

291

Every Couple Should Know...

a broken heart
leaves room
for God to enter.

———

292

Every Couple Should Know...

they need
a weekend retreat
at least twice a year.

293

Every Couple Should Know...

how to keep
from misinterpreting
your spouse's feelings.

294

Every Couple Should Know...

how to cure
your partner's headaches.

295

Every Couple Should Know...

honesty can hurt
but lying will scar.

296

Every Couple Should Know...

marriage is
a team sport.

297

Every Couple Should Know...

Cinderella and Prince Charming are fairy-tale characters.

298

Every Couple Should Know...

marriage is permanent but parenting is temporary.

Every Couple Should Know...

Hollywood romances
are not filmed
in the world of reality.

Every Couple Should Know...

to pray for
strength and sensitivity.

301

Every Couple Should Know...

to stop and
celebrate sunsets.

302

Every Couple Should Know...

there is nothing permanent
about a spouse...
except change.

Every Couple Should Know...

the incredible feeling
of true companionship.

Every Couple Should Know...

how to express
affection without
sexual expectation.

305

Every Couple Should Know...

your spouse's potential.

306

Every Couple Should Know...

you don't need to be embarrassed
about receiving professional help
for a marital tune-up.

307

Every Couple Should Know...

a healthy marriage
can make you something,
while a poor marriage
can reduce you to nothing.

308

Every Couple Should Know...

failure is a situation
and not a person.

309

Every Couple Should Know...

when to constructively criticize
and when to remain silent.

310

Every Couple Should Know...

Scripture's encouragement
for you to love your spouse
as Christ loved His church.

311

Every Couple Should Know...

how to put together
a first-class evening
for a first-class spouse.

312

Every Couple Should Know...

marriages rarely blow out...
they usually end
through slow leaks.

313

Every Couple Should Know...

how to
sexually surprise
your spouse.

314

Every Couple Should Know...

the best exercise
for the heart
is building up one another.

315

Every Couple Should Know...

how to make
the Christmas season
unforgettable.

316

Every Couple Should Know...

to keep intimate secrets
just that—secret.

317

Every Couple Should Know...

to not point out a fault
unless you are willing
to help your spouse
overcome it.

318

Every Couple Should Know...

when to back off.

Every Couple Should Know...

pride rests
at the root of
most marital conflicts.

Every Couple Should Know...

a good marriage is
the most rewarding form
of human intimacy.

321

Every Couple Should Know...

"Why are you so upset?"
is usually a dumb
and obvious question.

322

Every Couple Should Know...

that God can meet
every single one
of your needs.

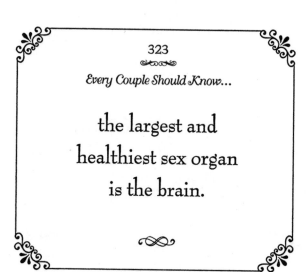

323

Every Couple Should Know...

the largest and
healthiest sex organ
is the brain.

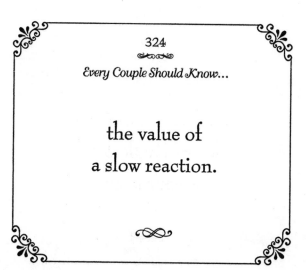

324

Every Couple Should Know...

the value of
a slow reaction.

325

Every Couple Should Know...

your spouse's fear
can turn into courage
with the right amount
of encouragement.

326

Every Couple Should Know...

the joy of making up
after a quarrel.

Every Couple Should Know...

sexual satisfaction was part
of God's design
for marriage.

Every Couple Should Know...

lasting relationships
don't just happen.

329

Every Couple Should Know...

television has a lethal gas
known to kill romance.

330

Every Couple Should Know...

there are many rich divorced
couples who would gladly
exchange their money
for their marriage.

331

Every Couple Should Know...

to ask for
your spouse's advice.

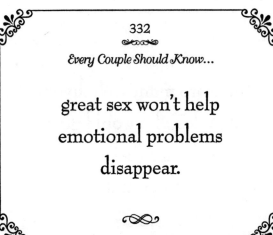

332

Every Couple Should Know...

great sex won't help
emotional problems
disappear.

333

Every Couple Should Know...

if your like for your spouse fades,
the love will soon die also.

334

Every Couple Should Know...

it's much easier to find
weaknesses than strengths.

Every Couple Should Know...

guidelines for a great
marriage won't work
unless you apply them.

Every Couple Should Know...

the importance of
appreciating the little things
your spouse does.

337

Every Couple Should Know...

it's better to ask
than to assume.

338

Every Couple Should Know...

it is more important
to understand
your spouse's feelings
than to explain them.

339

your spouse's needs
ought to come before
your personal activities.

340

how to express anger
without constantly saying
the word *you.*

Every Couple Should Know...

a man's sex drive
is similar to
a drum solo.

Every Couple Should Know...

a woman's sex drive
is similar to
a finely tuned orchestra.

343

Every Couple Should Know...

a few ways to catch
your spouse's interest.

344

Every Couple Should Know...

liking your spouse
is as important
as loving him or her.

345

Every Couple Should Know…

a man's knowledge
of his wife's real needs
is primitive.

346

Every Couple Should Know…

to work on
a few projects together.

347

Every Couple Should Know...

to refuse finding
sexual satisfaction
with others.

348

Every Couple Should Know...

to shatter the
superior versus
inferior roles.

349

Every Couple Should Know...

forgiveness is
a lifelong process.

350

Every Couple Should Know...

criticism isn't
an effective form
of foreplay.

351

Every Couple Should Know...

genuine love is
valuing a spouse
as God does.

352

Every Couple Should Know...

how to help each other
eat without spilling
while driving in the car.

353

Every Couple Should Know...

no matter how busy your
spouse is, he or she will always
have time for a favorite hobby.

354

Every Couple Should Know...

sexual desire
is not necessarily love.

Every Couple Should Know...

these four words
are dangerous:
I told you so.

Every Couple Should Know...

how to create
a sense of curiosity
before sharing
important information.

357

Every Couple Should Know...

the triggers
that hurt feelings.

358

Every Couple Should Know...

how to comfort with
gentleness and silence.

359

Every Couple Should Know...

the value of a hug.

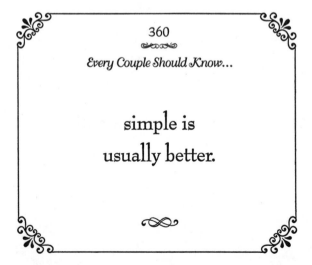

360

Every Couple Should Know...

simple is
usually better.

361

Every Couple Should Know...

the beautiful butterfly
was once a caterpillar.

362

Every Couple Should Know...

gratefulness expressed
through encouragement
is a strong motivator.

363

Every Couple Should Know...

to move
your primary focus
from your spouse to God.

364

Every Couple Should Know...

the more valuable
the possession,
the better
you care for it.

365

Every Couple Should Know...

your spouse

is priceless.

About the Author

Doug Fields, founder of YouthMinistryOnline.com, oversees student ministries at his church in California. He has written more than 20 books, speaks worldwide to youth workers, and teaches at Purpose-Driven Youth Ministry conferences. He holds an M.Div. from Fuller Theological Seminary. Happily married, Doug and his wife, Cathy, have three children, Torie, Cassie, and Cody, who provide many of his real-life illustrations.

Other Good
Harvest House Reading

100 Fun and Fabulous Ways to Flirt with Your Spouse
by Doug Fields

One hundred clever ideas, from foot massages to love notes to heart shaped pancakes, make it easy for couples celebrating a marriage or anniversary to ignite the spark of romance with flirtatious fun throughout the years.

Men Are Like Waffles—Women Are Like Spaghetti
by Bill and Pam Farrell

The authors explain why a man is like a waffle, why a woman is like spaghetti, and what these differences mean. With biblical insights, sound research, humorous anecdotes, and real-life stories, Bill and Pam Farrell show you how to achieve more satisfying relationships.

After You Say "I Do" Devotional
by H. Norman Wright

From creating special times together to finding harmony in your differences, the bestselling author of *Quiet Times for Couples* offers a wealth of practical ideas and suggestions you can use to bring more joy into your marriage and enrich your relationship.